THE

RUNNER

Books by Gary Gildner

Poetry

The Runner   1978
Letters from Vicksburg   1976
Nails   1975
Digging for Indians   1971
First Practice   1969

Anthology

Out of This World: Poems from the Hawkeye State
(with Judith Gildner)   1975

UNIVERSITY OF PITTSBURGH PRESS

THE RUNNER

Gary Gildner

Published by the University of Pittsburgh Press, Pittsburgh, Pa. 15260
Copyright © 1978, Gary Gildner
All rights reserved
Feffer and Simons, Inc., London
Manufactured in the United States of America

Library of Congress Cataloging in Publication Data

Gildner, Gary.
    The runner.

    (Pitt poetry series)
    I. Title.
PS3557.I343R8   811'.5'4   77-14692
ISBN 0-8229-3365-9
ISBN 0-8229-5291-2 pbk.

Some of the poems in this book first appeared in *Aisling, The American Review, fiction international, Granite, Kansas Quarterly, New Letters,* and *Poetry Northwest.* The "Letters from Vicksburg" were first published in *Antaeus.* "The Runner" first appeared in *The Paris Review.* "Statistics," "The High Class Bananas," "The Picnic," and "Breaking Bones" first appeared in *Poetry Now.*

"Then" copyright © 1977 by Gary Gildner. Reprinted from *Fifty Contemporary Poets: The Creative Process,* edited by Alberta Turner. Copyright © 1977 by David McKay Company, Inc.; copyright © 1977 by Longman Inc. Reprinted by permission of Longman Inc. and the author.

Thanks are due to Yaddo, where some of these poems were written.

for Judy

. . . and just as we was leaving I found a tolerable good curry-comb, and Jim he found a ratty old fiddle-bow, and a wooden leg. The straps was broke off of it, but barring that, it was a good enough leg, though it was too long for me and not long enough for Jim, and we couldn't find the other one, though we hunted all around.

— Huck Finn

CONTENTS

PART 1

THEN

In the village the children
were what they had always been —
a girl wanted to be a nurse
or a dancer, a boy wished for a horse
or an elephant up in his bed.
Autumn got chilly, winter hard
and longer than dreams, but dreams
came back, slippery and quick
as minnows. And spring —
spring made you stop, look,
and fall from the sky
for keeps. You had a tadpole
and the whole day . . .
One summer, tasting the salt
on your lips, you promised forever —
and the cricket's song was long and full
before it got slimmer and quit.
But the road and the river
were what they always had been,
and your heart would not break, not ever.

THE RUNNER

Show the runner coming through the shadows,
   show him falling into a speckled rhythm,
   and then show the full expression of light,
   there, where the trees quit and the road
   goes on alone, marked by the moon-glazed gravel

Show the runner trying to disappear
   where sky and road meet far in the distance,
   show him always a step too late,
   show a train going by hauling a long silence,
   and show the runner leaving the road
   where the killdeer starts from a charred stump

Show the runner saying the names of streams
   as if he were working off days in purgatory,
   show the Chocolay, the Rifle, the Fox,
   the Laughing Whitefish, the Escanaba,
   show the runner's pocketful of worms
   and show the runner's father
   sitting alone by a hole in the ice

Show the runner stopping at farm after farm
   until a woman appears who is wearing a child's
   pink kimono over her shoulders,
   show her feet in hunting socks,
   a kitchen arranged in cream and linoleum,
   show that the wind has toasted her cheeks,
   show that she doesn't know what he wants

Show the runner's old room, the crucifix
   he tied fresh palms around each year,
   the five nice birch his father planted,
   the two blue spruce, the silver maple,
   the cherry from the nursery that was going broke,
   the man who said take it for a buck,
   the hail storm that knocked them over

Show the runner setting out all spruced up,
   show the sun, poached, above a grove of leggy birch,
   show the runner cruising down a cow path
   trying to catch his breath,
   and show the slim white limbs dividing
   letting him in

Show the runner peeling bark
   and scratching messages with sticks,
   then show him diving into a drift,
   nosing like a mole out of season,
   rolling over and over
   and yipping for luck or in pain

Show the runner approach the only light
   in Little Lake, there, over the grocer's
   fading pack of Camels,
   show the grocer chewing Red Man,
   listen to him play his pocket change
   and resurrect the dead,
   listen to him spit them back

Show the runner running on,
   show the moon, then show it stalking him
   across the road into the second growth,
   show the runner's father in his garden
   blue and out of breath and looking hard
   at something nothing can distract him from,
   show the lake all frozen over,
   show the mound of snow

JOHANN GAERTNER (1793–1887)

In the blue winter of 1812
Johann Gaertner, a bag of bones,
followed Napoleon home.
He was cold; Napoleon,
riding ahead under a bear
wrap, fumed at the lice
in his hair.   — From Moscow
to Borodino, from Borodino
to the Baltic Sea, Napoleon
fumed and slapped, and glared hard
at the gray shapes
pushing at his face.
And maybe ate a piece of fruit
he did not taste. If he
cried, we do not know it.
But Johann Gaertner, 19,
a draftee, a bag of bones,
blew on his fingers
and bit them, and kicked at his toes.
And chewed and chewed
a piece of pony gristle.
And once, trying to whistle
an old dog into his coat,
swallowed a tooth.
God save Johann! Johann
Gaertner, 19, cried,
moving his two blue feet
through bloody holes his eyes
kept staring and staring at . . .
And in the midst of all this
one night God appeared, hoary and fat,
and yelled at him in Russian,
Kooshat! Kooshat! —
and Johann closed his eyes

6

waiting for one of his sharp white bones
to pierce his heart.
When none did, he dragged them
past the mirror Napoleon
gazed and gazed at his rasp-
berry-colored chin in . . .
and past windy St. Helena
where his former leader was already lost
among the washed-up herring.
And Johann kept going,
picking up crumbs like a sparrow! —
no longer hearing that tooth
grinding against his ribs,
but starting to feel the sun
on the back of his neck
for a change, and loving the itch
and salty wash of sweat
everywhere on his chest.
          And one day
holding up a jug of cool switchel,
he had swig upon swig upon swig
and felt his whole blessed mouth
turn ginger —
and he whispered a song
that came out *Ah, Johann* . . .
          Thus,
having stopped, he stepped back
and took in his fields of hay,
his acres and acres of feed,
and his six black bulls
bulging against the sky.
And sitting down he ate
the giant mounds of sweet
red cabbage his ample wife

7

set before him,
and the pickled corn,
and the mashed potatoes dripping
galaxies of gizzards, hearts,
and juicy bits of wing,
and yet another slice
of her salt-rising bread
spread with his own
bee-sweetened butter.
(Often Johann stretched out big
in the clover, listening to his bees,
churn, churn, they said, *churn* . . .)
And praising God while licking his fingers
he allowed for a wedge of her
sour cream raisin pie,
and a mug of steaming
coffee out on the porch,
where he liked to stick his stockinged feet
among the fireflies,
and feel the slow closing
of his eyes . . .
                    And all of this
(including the hickory-nut cake,
rhubarb wine, and the fine old fat-
bellied kitchen stove)
happened for many years
in little Festina, Iowa, —
where Anton Dvorak came to drink
local Bohemian beer
and hear the Turkey River;
and where rosy Johann Gaertner
dug down deep in the rich black dirt
to make his own hole
and one for his wife as well.

8

TODAY THEY ARE ROASTING
ROCKY NORSE

Today they are roasting Rocky Norse.
Me, today they are roasting me
while I sit here, dead from the belt down.
But hey! Look at these trousers. Black Nickle
born with a ball in his palms, Mr. Real Fine Hands,
he'd say Man those are fly pants, man. Fly.
& wiggle both flat hands down by his hams
cooling everything. Black Nickle. Who came in grim & gray
when they propped me up in all those good pillows, all that
pretty gash flashing their choppers around my head, pop, pop
ROCKY NORSE IS FIGHTING BACK. Gray, man, he was *ash*.

I like pork, always have. Smell it boys
& tell me what is better, clean sweat pants
or a woman from South Dakota — from someplace
you never heard of — keeping it warm in the parking lot.
Her old man raised sheep but she raised the moon
raised it up & gave it over. Fly, Mr. Rocky.
Or clean socks & no god damn throbbing
knees & shoulders when it rains.
I'll tell you what I liked about that woman.
She could drive all day over South Dakota
& two more hours over Minnesota
& still raise the moon soft & mellow.

I remember one time I looked in the sky over Red Oak
& he threw me a horse-wink, the grinning fool.
Another time grabbing that salamander,
it was so orange she wanted to eat it.
Pump pump went its throat. Pump pump pump.
Finally I put it down. Go on, get out of here.
Go raise some big kids that can tackle.
South Dakota said Rocky you are my man.
South Dakota said that, her & her funny dreams.

9

Somewhere water's dripping on a sink full of nylons.
Another beer? Sure, give it here. & when my baggie's full
kid you can empty it, how's that? Today is my day.
Roasting Rocky. & the smoke going up from that hog
is going up all over the Midwest, going up over St. Cloud
Bemidji & even Dee-troit where Snake hauled his buns
out of & tore over my ass one time so quick & beautiful
nothing would ever stop him & nothing did, the greaser
safety wet his pants just straining to watch I believe.

What was that dream she had down in Dallas? God yes
she said Rocky you carried around a sack of darkness
like a sack of black dirt & you tied it next to your belly.
I said how about a sack of money honey, but she went on
those green eyes big & wide & all that red hair falling
everywhere, saying I laid down with it & stroked the folds
like I wanted it to take me in.

Wake up baby, I am here! ROCKY NORSE the sign says
& the arrow is pointing straight at that hog
I am getting the first piece of. Free.
Along with all the Hamms I can pour in my baggie.
& everyone's shown up except those two bastards
who were raised on ears & lips & parts
no one can stand to even look at.
But I guess I spook Nickle
& maybe Snake is dead. Which I can say I am glad
I am not. Hey listen. All that sponge they cut from my knees,
what difference does it make to me now?

You get used to everything. If I could do it
without spitting up all over my tie
I'd lead a cheer. OK fans

gimme ah *you!*
gimme ah *get!*
gimme ah *get-used-to-EVERYTHING!*

South Dakota swing your smooth moon up here
next to my King Daddy Seat of Honor
& tell the folks about that seed you
found on the sheet between your dimpled knees.
What'd it look like baby?
A kidney bean Rocky & it was breathing
I wanted to put it back in
but I couldn't & I couldn't
find anyone who would
I touched it Rocky
& it stopped breathing
a piece of paper, that's all it was
a piece of paper folded in half
no, I opened it up
Rocky it was a plastic sack
you were inside
all of your little pieces . . .

My first bike was a fat-tired job the Red Oak
Sears had to special order. & I know exactly
where that bike is today, it's frozen under
Crab Smoltz's hog barn. When they were all
standing around with their little pliers fixing my spine
I saw that fat-tired honey rising up shiny & new
from the wet cement I pushed it into, rising up
with the first good man who ever taped my ankles
glued to the seat & twisting those grips for
all he was worth, saying Rocky I got this machine

but it's too much! Take it off my hands!
So I took that shiny Red Flyer off Coker's
small swift hands & rose up past Crab Smoltz's
sun-roasted face & his hogs that looked just like him
& up past my old man saying quit running
those cows when they're full god dammit
up past Snake & South Dakota up past Nickle up past
the Mayflower truck that wouldn't move & the long
white line I laid my nose against thinking this is one
godawful wrong place to fall off
my brand new Harley & cream . . .

I think when God sits back & looks
at everything he made he gets
a hole in his gut.
I broke everything — neck & legs & both cheeks.
& buried half a chopper in my tongue.
Hey God you ever feel like a jerk?
You ever feel looking down at this handsome boy
who could open up holes for semis
who's got to tickle out his own crap now —
you ever feel like calling in sick?

Religion, my old man said he had all of it
he needed in two hundred head & no TB.
My mother went when somebody croaked. & baked something.
Snake said don't knock it man.
Right baby I don't knock it, I eat pork
I eat the hog you are not here to see my name on
along with all the boys & their trim women
who cut it up in little pieces
at twenty-five bucks a plate,
along with South Dakota & her red hair
falling all over those white shoulders.

I am eating pork with a hole in my tongue
hey Snake I am going down, my juice baby
my meat are making muscle. Tearing open
those slots baby, moving everything to one side
& coming back where they don't see us
they don't see us Snake but they smell something
real good going up over Red Wing going up
over Shenandoah over Winona over Dallas & New York City
they want in baby they are screaming their guts out
they want in so bad . . .

They want in where the water won't
quit dripping baby tell them how it is.
Tell them you are my turtle
you save my legs from the sharks.
But please don't say my heart is a peach
my heart is a bag of nuts somebody cut off
one of Crab's pigs, milky blue blood
is pumping it baby milky blue blood
tell them

WHEN THE RETARDED SWIM

at the Y on Fridays
a lot of time is taken up
with holding them, so they do not drown.
They whoop and squeal, they sound
like children given some wine
with their bread, but their bones
will not follow smoothly
where the flesh wants them to.
The retarded enter the water like cattle,
slowly, led down a sloping gangway
by a man with a full, curly beard.
He makes them bellow — their large eyes
dart in every direction, their feet
think the water is fire, or Jello,
or something else altogether lovely.
Some of the men get erections
and thrash at toys the attendants
have set to bobbing, their pink eyes
made pinker by chlorine,
and two or three of the women
find squiggly fish in their suits
and are beside themselves with joy . . .
and no one ever wants to go.
Outside, miles away, it may be
October or the dead of winter.
Leaves clutter an old man's walk
or snow lies frozen under a sparrow's
peck and weave. Wetting a finger
the old man discovers which way
the wind wants to blow his fire,

and the sparrow suddenly flies away
toward another part of the city,
where it is summer — where a young boy,
his eager hands far too small,
bobbles a ball —
                   But he runs after it.

FINGERS

When Ronald, Mr. Lacey's son, came home from the war, he showered, put on a pair of new jeans and a new T-shirt, found his old high-school baseball cap and pulled it down snug over his forehead, then went outside and shot baskets. He shot baskets for about two weeks. One day Mr. Lacey said, "What about that money you saved up? What are you going to do with it?" Ronald shot baskets for a while longer, then went downtown and bought an old Hudson Hornet. He spent five days driving the Hudson back and forth through town, stopping for a root beer when he got thirsty. On the sixth day, when a tire went flat, Ronald locked the car and put his thumb in the air. The next day in the Atkins Museum in Kansas City, he bought a dozen picture postcards of Houdon's bust of Benjamin Franklin, because with that bald top and that long hair in back that fell to his shoulders, Franklin looked like the queerest duck he'd ever seen. Also Franklin seemed peeved about something. Then Ronald took a bus to New York City. The ride was nothing to crow about — and for maybe three hundred miles a man next to him wanted to describe losing his prostate gland. In New York, Ronald found a room a stone's throw from Yankee Stadium. He sent one of the Franklin cards to his father, saying only "Love, Ronald." Then he sat looking out the window. On the fire escape was a piece of red balloon that the wind was trying to blow away. Finally the wind succeeded and Ronald was tired. He took off his clothes, climbed into bed, and began to count the fingers on his shooting hand.

PART II

Seventeen of the poems in this section are based on a series of letters written by a Union soldier to his wife in Iowa. The man spelled pretty much by ear, often employing *t* for *d* or *s* (writing *hat* for *had*, for example, and *Divition* for *Division*), and he used no punctuation — the letters simply run on, broken up only by occasional paragraphing (here and there I have used extra spacing to indicate pauses and stops). I tried to remain faithful to this grammar, especially when a phrase like "scars of amunition" — meaning "scarce of ammunition" — occurred. The last poem is based on a letter from an officer — found with the soldier's — and I tried to keep his formality. I view these eighteen sonnets as translations, even though I did not use all of the original material and departed from it whenever it seemed necessary or fruitful.

G. G.

LETTERS FROM VICKSBURG

I

Aprile the 17/63

Dear woman I am well and hope you ar
the same   to tell you wher we ar will be
a mater prety hard for I dont hartly
now my self   but now the River is not far
we hav to stop and fix the leavy ther
at Carthage wher we aim the enemy
is fortifying   fifteen hundret men
we hav forty thousand here and one
hole Divition has been promised soon
they want to kep us out of Jackson Miss
if we can cut the Rebels off from ther
in Vicksburgh we will giv them holy thud
well I must hury up and finish this
the boys ar well and in good hart   John Blood

II

May the 7/63

Dear woman I was glat to hear from you
yours of Aprile 29 and glat
to hear that you was well and Edward to
we hav hat hart fighting sins we crost
the Missippi   many maimed and lost
a plan to martch was met by Rebels near
Port Gibson   they was in a canebrake ther
we hat to drive them out with beyonet
witch we don with fulsom sped and got them
on the open field wher we shot them
down by hundrets but they stot thair ground til
noon   they tried retreat   we charged and killed
til sunset   Captain Staley lost his sord
and I my cap for witch I thank the Lord

III

We left the River seven days ago
with 3 days Rations   sins our battel
I hav hartly climed down from my satel
looking for a bite   2 days ago
12 miles from Camp our squat came to a nise
plantation with a grove around it and
a hedge   so that the inmates of the house
dit not notise our aprotch   when they
saw us stanting at the dore they jumped
and screamed   I told them they neat not be scart
for we was only yankey soldiers only
hungry and was never nowen to hert
the ladies   so we took posesion of
the tabel ate a harty dinner   then
helpt ourselfs to other things we wanted

IV

May the 8/63

Dear woman I again take pen in hand
to let you now that I am well this day
I hav nothing new to write   we stand
mutch nearer Vicksburgh in a redish clay
in a line of battel sevrel miles
up and down a creek   we heare the Rebels
plan to meat us here and meat us ther and
I dont giv a blast   sixty thousand men
stand by tonight and we expect to be
reanforsed to twise that by tomorrow
I hat ment befor to tell you that we
use the Zouave Drill   laying down to load
ther by saving many men the hollow
road   the male mule is here   goodby   John Blood

V

May the 17/63

Dear woman I am sor a littel bit
but I will tel you some thing of our martch
to Vicksburgh yesterday   befor I quit
to sleep   the boys hav not hat mutch
we hat just come off a suny field
when they hit and cut us all to peases
I never notised the retreat at first
every thing was falling thick with dust
the men all jumped into a ditch and layed
down   and fired onse or twise   I jumped in
and fired onse or twise and looked around
to see what all the boys was doing now
being that the shooting stoped   and they was
running fast but for a few that huncked
the ground and wept as close as posable

VI

Dear wife I feal prety rested now
and wil continue with my pen   I said
the Rebels hat us close and hot and how
I got away with all thair balls so hard
behind was I just ran   and just as I
got to the Regiment Sam Hamitt fell
hit 2 plases   thro the breast and thro the thi
he lost his head and begged for me to make him well
I dragged him to a plase of shelder
in the shade ther he was out of danger
then I wiped his fase but dont
now what he tried to say   the Rebels hat thair
guns on me   I let them hav the contents
of my own and ran   not nowing wher I went

VII

Dear wife and friend I dozed but now will try
to finish this   I wanderd in the thick
until my hart sloed down   I hat to ty
my foot   for I hat looked and seen the slick
collecting ther along my boot   they shot
my big toe off   also I was struck
with grape against the neas   my pants wer cut
by glancing balls which left me welds on both
my angels   God hat bilt me tall enough
I gess   I herd a halt   to my surprise
General Logan and his forse of seven
thousand stot beyond the treas   O Heaven
help the Rebels now   I hureyed up to him
and said our men wer going down like flys

VIII

I went with General Logans men and we
confused the Rebels so they jumped around
and did not now witch end to pick   see
we hat them in a pintch   and then we made
a charge with beyonets   a few wer ful
of furie yet but Logans men wer fresh
and yeled like farm boys raising gutsie Hell
at gelding time   2,000 prisoners
we took   I helped to make them safe   one cursed
my other foot but he hat such a mess
about his ear and fase I payed no mind
I hat to go back on the Battel ground
in serch of my own Regiment   my feet
steped over deat and wounted thick as sheep

IX

May the 27/63
at Vicksburgh

Dear wife and friend I hav not mutch to write
for it has only been a steady rore
of muskets canons mortars and just mor
of that sins the begining of our fight
on the 16th   no telling when the scrape
of shels will end or how   the Rebels ar
surroundet so they cant with lif escape
our line of battels over ten miles long
gunboats guart the River and our trench
is all the way around thair forts   a pintch
so close they cant get to thair canons
if any one will show himself we sling
the balls out after him and black him down
my love to you   my sheat has no mor room

X

Dear loved one well the last 2 days I spent
down in the trenches   now Im out and dont
feal mutch like writing letters on account
of not mutch sleep   but I should tell you what
I mean by beaing in the trenches
I mean by beaing in the trenches that
a ditch was dug in clear around the fort
within a hundret yards of them   and that
we hav our batrees planted in the trench
behind us throwing shels up in thair fort
all the time we throw the shels in   in fact
they must be getting scars of amunition
for I hav not heart over 3 reports
from them sins I am in my station

XI

Dear loved one did I mention General Grants
trik he pulled on Rebel General Johnston
when we captured Jackson   well he sents
a telegraph   sent him amunition
quik   for them Damd yankeys ar acomin
then he sined it with the Rebel Generals name
when the train pulled into Edwarts station
loaded down with shels and canon balls we
captured it   so I think thair artilry
is about played out   I may be rong   jokes
can turn against you   but I hope its true
weve only lost 4 men sins coming heare
2 of them by bad shels from our own
I sent my love to you and all your folks

XII

Dear wife and bosom friend I hat seen hart
sites befor I ever saw a battel
field   at Edwarts station hospitel
I fount out what it was to see a hert
the one that makes me dry hat lost his tong
the ball past thro his teeth and cut it off
and made his eyes and everything look rong
but heare theres times with the secesh thats grate
we dont shoot at them after dark and they
of corse dont shoot at us   the moon shines so
that we can see each other plain as day
we hav the right to go half ways acrost
and they can come half ways acrost to us
we leave our arms and some come cleare acrost

XIII

June the 6/63
Camp SE of Vicksburgh

Dear Cecelia well its shel and shel and
welcom mor deserters evry night   they
tell us they get just a litel corn bread
and thair amunitions low   I can say
another thing   that when the win blows on us
from that way we cant stay put   because it
stinks so bat   no ones hert and 2 ar sick
the Lutenant has the peevish diaree
the Sergent has Consumption and the flux
well I dont now whi you dont write to me
I hav to write and do write evry chance
I get   I dont now wether you dont write
or wether I dont get them in this plase

XIV

Dear Cecelia we hav hat some warm times
in the Company sins last I wrote to you
on Monday the Lutenant died   and Sims
first Corprel died of feaver   and a slew
of other vakancys ar coming up
as officers receive paroll   the way
we fil them is by vote   well the question
of Lutenant laid between Lon Baily
and myself   only Colonel Connell hat
promised Baily and he fount out if he
left it to the vote whi I would get three
forth   so he sent rite strate for Bailys bars
now he wants to make me sargent   well heres
what I want   nothing   if it aint by vote

XV

Some boys ar playing cards but I dont feal
like it   it is a prety night altho
the stink is bat   to bat the win cant blow
the other way   or rain a bit and peal
off thair scud   they hav horses mules and cows
runing round thair forts and when they get to
neare we shoot them   dogs or anything   a sows
thair now that they could surely put to
use   but it wont help a thing except I
gess the ground   and this grounds rich enough
talk is they hav hopes of General Johnston
coming in our rear to help them out   rough
chance of that   in the mean time if they try
to bury aney stinking corps we shoot them

XVI

July the 24/63
Millikens Bend La

Dear and most Loved wife it is with pleasure
I sit up to write you   but I cant say
I am well this time   I hav hat Chill feaver
ever sins I wrote you last   yesterday
I did not hav it   or today yet   plus
I am in hopes I hav it broke   dear mate
I hope this finds you well and Eddie to
I have not hat a singel letter from you
for a month   o you dont now how   anctious
I can feal   one come to the 28th
and my brother sent it on to Vicksburgh
but the man he sent it by he never
gave it to me   it is lost   and aney
way I gess hes gone with Grant to Georgy

XVII

July the 31/63
Millinkens Bend La

Dear and Mutch Loved One with pleasure I take
my pen and opertunity to let
you now Im still among the living but
not well   I hat Chill feaver   hat that broke
then took a bat dyree witch I cant stop
all the metacen dont seem to help
it only helps to weaken me to sor
but I would like so mutch to now whi I
dont get a letter from you aney mor
if you decitet you dont want to write
me aney mor just let me now   be shore
to anser this one soon   if in a short
time I dont heal I shal try to land
a furlow and come home   goodby   John Blood

XVIII

Berwick La.
Oct 2nd 1863

Mrs. Blood. Dear Madam, Yours of Sept. 13
arrived to hand last night. I must be mean.
We had for some time previous no word
from your good husband, one of Iowa's
brave sons. Then we had the word that he was
coming back. As time went on no further word
from John until a week ago we heard
that he had died aboard the "R. C. Wood"
of Typhoid fever August 4. I have sent
his final statements and his military
history on to Washington D.C. Truly
I assure you, Madam, I was hurt,
for John was hardy, in the best of health —
but O alas! in life we are in death.

PART III

4th BASE

Decked out in flannels and gripping my mitt
I was running laps, long grassy laps,
and hearing my 200 bones start to chatter —
I had finally arrived in the major leagues!

I stopped in the infield, dropping
to a shoulder stand — my big toes pointing out the sun! —
and there was no pain, even at 37.

Then we started to play — I was at 4th —
and my first throw over to 1st
bounced in on the 10th or 11th dribble.

Odd, I thought,
that the game had developed such wrinkles.
But shuck that, I was here now, bounding
around my sack like a well-oiled seal, barking
"Dust everyone off! Dust everyone off!"

After a while I slipped into Mass
and sat with my old teammates —
the ones from high school who had grown pink
and jowly, and who played with their keys
between their knees, and who
when the choir leaned forward to sing our song
covered their eyes, and mumbled, and wouldn't look at me.

HARRY JAMES & THE UNTUNED PIANO

Harry it's a great thrill to shake that mitt
   here in the Hawkeye State I've shaken
   the Count's the Duke's the fabulous Louis
   Bellson's from little Moline on the river
   but this is an honor a kick
   I can't tell you

Thank you it's nice

And the folks Harry they loved you out there
   all the old tunes Carnegie Hall
   You Made Me Love You
   Harry too bad about that piano Harry

Aw man

I don't suppose over the years Helen O'Connell
   Vegas Betty Grable you bump into
   what's the word I want Harry

Aw man when a fine piano player like
   you know Jack sits down

No kidding I'll bet that fried the band
   for a loop those pickled notes
   you practice much Harry
   work out I mean on last week's
   show we talked with the great

I practice sure I practice

I'll bet you had to scrap some numbers
   change the book hubba hubba
   Harry what about Hollywood

Look I've got a sore tooth
   can the radio audience see these gums
   the people loved us we play for the people

I ached for you Harry I hurt
   is this your first time
   through Iowa Harry

Once a year the people love us
   popcorn catfish bad pianos
   you roll with the punch
   a nice crowd small but nice

I'll bet this trip is embedded
   Harry how's Jack
   I'll bet he's beer & cold cuts Harry

Listen that particular box was
   I'll tell you about bad boxes
   I mean stinko fella that was a *good*
   OK piano baby very nice

How about getting started Harry
   your big break Betty
   the kids our listeners

I was playing baseball

Baseball Harry

Beaumont Texas American Legion
   we play for the people
   hockey marbles hotdogs
   name your poison
   we play for the people

THE PAGE TURNER

Anonymous, she takes her chair
beside the bench on which the French
piano player sits, arranging his hands.
She wears a yellow dress,
and her face is flushed the color
love composes, waiting for him,
and the flutist, to begin.
Her own hands hold each other.
Then the world, wakened,
hears its first bright noises —
leaning forward she is quick to follow:
they are on a river riding over shallows,
over morning mist toward its source.
Each time she turns a page
she feels a minnow brush her fingertips.
But here is where the world starts
to take her, where the river narrows
to a rapids — here
among the flecks of sunlight bouncing
off the rocks, off the backs of flickers diving
past her shoulders, off the leaves
gathered, swirling, in a pool.
She is all alone and doesn't know it —
doesn't know her body's free,
nor that she's found the falls
the flutist moving faster almost dancing
and the French piano player in his madness
to control the birds his hands have turned into
have given her, alone, among a thousand nervous witnesses.
Nor later when she tries to sleep beyond her tears
will she know that joy applauds
and loves her for her frailty.

THE HIGH-CLASS BANANAS

The bananas down at the Safe Way
were doing OK last week, just as
they'd been doing all along probably,
just lying around on the wood bench
waiting for folks to come by &
look over what they'd like sliced up
on their Grape Nuts in the morning,
or in their raspberry Jello at night,
or maybe what they'd go for after school, plain,
with a big glass of nice cold sweet milk
— to get away from questions like
"How many lights are now on in the 1st place?"
or that other devil, "The fountain pen
was invented 1 century and 1 year
after the balloon. In what year
was the fountain pen invented?"
No, nobody had a lot of grief
over the bananas down at the Safe Way,
not the way they just lay there
waiting for you, wanting to make you feel good.
Then somebody, maybe somebody who *knew*
how many lights were now on in the 1st place,
got to thinking, Hey!
why don't we get a merry-go-round
down at the Safe Way? A big red carousel
that makes a little pizzaz? a little hubba hubba?
& put the bananas on it! & stick some plastic
leaves on top! & some fuzzy monkeys!
& some palm trees! & everybody pushed up close
said Yeah! They said Yeah! Yeah!
& so now we got high-class bananas
going round & round down at the Safe Way.
& you stand there, maybe scratching where it itches,
waiting for your bunch to come around.

LIFE & DEATH IN SKOKIE

However it began, it began almost at once —

He would dress her up like a little Greenland doll
    & kiss the insides of her elbows,
    the tops of her knees
    & then, as if lost in a howling storm,
    drift into sleep.

She would find notes he had left marking his place
    in adventure stories, books he would never finish;
    always they said, "I have never sizzled."

He would stand in a cold telephone booth, his wisdom
    tooth aching, & listen to her hum.

She would follow him to a bar in a foreign neighborhood
    & while he sat in the back under a rack of antlers
    she would slip down beside his tires
    & let all the air out.

He would bump her begonia off the antique whatnot,
    scuff his loafers in the dirt,
    then make tracks for the club
    where he worked on his old windup
    & practiced approaching the net.

She would draw his funny bone in charcoal
    then rub it, ferociously, until her cheeks burned.

He would eat a celery stick
    & slap the latest averages.

She would read the life of Edward Hopper, the life
    of Kierkegaard, the life of Fanny Brice,
    & crack Brazil nuts, almonds, or chew ice.

He would open his eyes in the middle of the night
    & declare he only wanted a mountain life,
    declare he only wanted to raise goats & have a wife
    wake him up nights when mice scrapped in the rafters.

She would promise to can his pumpkins.

He would promise to churn the earth.

She would say, "But something else is trying to surface . . ."

He would say, "But something else is trying to roll free . . ."

THE CONSUMER

Hung over the upholstered pot
he was feeling not so hot.

Not a drop
of pick-up.

Nor a new screen
to sift for nuggets in his chunky refuse, even.

And when someone near & dear
offered him a year-

old thing
to fondle, it to kicking

in the nuts his television
was akin

— so confused
was he, & disconnected.

Somehow, though,
he passed the night, & this morning oh

boy! picked him up a bunch of motherhutch-
in Ethyl, Jack, & lettin pop the clutch

he is whoom!
he is handsome!

STATISTICS

"They say that couples who've been married five years don't talk to each other more than twenty-seven minutes a week." — overheard

Statistics say the heart is a long-stemmed glass
   you happen across after the party has busted up,
   that red wine crusted over the lip the kiss
   you once felt down to your toes, down where
   the minnows poured themselves into a giant silver drop

Statistics say we are sprouting stiff black bristles
   in all the places where we used to blush

Statistics say you will break six geranium pots
   in the seventh year, on the morning of the eighth
   you will catch yourself boring a hole
   above the old one, the one that never filled up,
   standing on slivers of wishbones

Statistics say the bears in the zoo
   scratch and yawn but they won't sleep with you

Statistics say no matter how many bottles you toss in the water,
   no matter how many loops you scoop, the milkpods you puffed
   out your cheeks for, flying and flying,
   are gone, along with the grandpas
   pulling the covers up over their chins

Statistics say you will quit walking barefoot
   the summer your name disappears from the sand

Statistics say please or listen once too often
   and then they forget and say it again,
   and we always hear them, that's the wonderful part,
   and then we forget and they repeat it, slowly,
   only we are bending closer to the mirror by now
   arranging something we want just so

STORY

She was lonely in the mirror
so she married, had a child

— named him for a soldier,
for a poet. She was pretty

and her soldier-poet boy had smoky hair,
smeared jelly on the face of old despair

— finger-painted
gray despair.

And so despair
fell down a well

just like a sow in summer,
like a salty sow.

And so they drank the rain
and in the forest

found a nest.
And Dog he came to live with them.

And Dog he wore a fine wool vest
and she a wedding dress.

LAST ARTICLES

Here is his coat;
hang it up
for the crows,
its histories
all have the same name:
wanting sun,
wanting rain.

Here the shirt,
its finest sweat
has turned into bright
pockets of heart-salt.
Hand it down
to an only son.

Here the pants —
there is a braggart inside
who could never help it.
Tear them into rags
to dust the piano,
the clock.

Finally the shoes,
those sad dependable cows
who traveled the same path
day after day
and said nothing.
Put them out in the orchard
where sparrows play.

PART IV

MY FATHER AFTER WORK

Putting out the candles
I think of my father asleep
on the floor beside the heat,
his work shoes side by side
on the step, his cap
capping his coat on a nail,
his socks slipping down,
and the gray hair over his ear
marked black by his pencil.

Putting out the candles
I think of winter, that quick
dark time before dinner
when he came upstairs after
shaking the furnace alive,
his cheek patched with soot,
his overalls flecked with
sawdust and snow,
and called for his pillow,
saying to wake him
when everything was ready.

Putting out the candles
I think of going away
and leaving him there,
his tanned face turning
white around the mouth,
his left hand under his head
hiding a blue nail,
the other slightly curled
at his hip, as if
the hammer had just
fallen out of it
and vanished.

THE PICNIC

The milkweed we picked last summer is holding
its own in my daughter's fallen-down castle
of ribbons and clippings of cats and koalas,
of hairpins and marbles and skinned crayolas

— despite the fact we ignored all the wisdom
to go in and give it a coat of hair spray,
not too close, that'll cream
the parachutes for sure. For sure,

I thought, but I'm not inflicting any
Twirl or Curl on those fragile prayers,
not sober, drunk, or inspired:
we picked that stalk

with our bare hands: and the pod,
round and firm and fully packed,
rode home in Judy's basket: bounced along,
I say, like a young tit.

*

Once addressing myself to a circle
of nuns on the subject of rime
and rhythm I blushed, thinking back
to a picture of Popeye's Olive Oyl

taking Popeye by the stalk: years ago
at the junior-high Halloween picnic.
Who had it?
Jenny Dyson, later spurred by a zoot

suit dandy with a lavender ragtop to drop
out of Latin, Band, Math, Religion
and all the rest, certainly had it:
a motion that drove us: the cleanest,

meanest, slickest, most dyna-flowing nun-
busting walk down the halls of Holy Redeemer
any of us had ever witnessed, and with which
my dreams are still, if they're lucky, tickled.

But no, she didn't spring the filthy Olive
and Popeye upon us: Catholic youth smacking
down apples and cider: then who?
My guess is Grab-Ass Gulick the Polish Mantis

(and for all those times he flicked at our jewels
I pray he got himself a proper mantis bride
who took her time): it was awful:
our first piece of porn: but the swift

kick it gave us into the world: the bulge
of knowledge to pit against Mary and
Joseph, Angels and Rainbows: Jenny's walk
even paled beside it and that was a shame —

instead of delight in the flight of that
marvelous engine, the air it displaced,
the sway of its parts that were one
part and proved itself simply by moving

we lusted to grab it, strip it, gum it
to death the way my neighbor's giant tortoise
gums lettuce hearts, then pees a quart: O
the old toothless dance, the routine rag . . .

*

And now on my window ledge a grackle knocks
a pair of sparrows off the suet ball
fastened there to attract song:
imagine writing the Ninth Symphony

and not being able to hear it: or worse
imagine spending the rest of your life
locked in a discount store in a heavy
coat that you can't take off: and tiny hairs

keep itching your neck and back — like those
you always brought home from the barber shop —
and the white, white fluorescent lights
that hum and hum can never be dimmed

or even made to quit: but you can lean
over, bob your head, and gobble all the gold-
fish that wiggle through and, aiming vaguely
at the monkey pellets, bite the dust.

                    *

I wish I knew what happened to Christina,
the German lady who lived with us when I was five
or six: she had one eye, like a pike on the wall,
and a brother who goose-stepped for Hitler:

I thought they meant he stepped on geese
because when his name came up it made her cry.
One time Grandpa and I left her and my
sister in the truck and took our onion

sandwiches and beer back in the woods: we found
a place where deer had rubbed the grass
away, unlaced our hightops, burped and became
two chunky gentlemen enjoying their estates:

and smack in the midst of our leak a fawn
all spindly poked its black eyes through
the pines and looked at us: going back
Grandpa said that women didn't like the woods,

it made them fuss: in the truck I saw
the truth of that: Christina had her missal
open on her lap and whispered from it
like the bears would eat her up for supper . . .

❀

O the green wothe botheth and the snow flea feeds
on diatoms as well as on other springtails:
I hated memorizing things in school
but go ahead, let's have some edification —

ask me what'll oviposit only on an aster
or who could play the field like Hoot Evers,
or who really saved beautiful Jane by swinging
across the piranha-mean Amazon to the far

hayloft in his grandfather's rickety barn
scrambling a nest of saber-toothed mice in the bargain:
or who's got the only milkweed pod on the block
that's blooming this winter, amazing
a family of mammals for absolutely nothing.

MY GERMAN GRANDMA

kept close tabs
on everything and
everything stayed
in its place —
the chairs,
the shiny wax
bananas, pears,
a cactus someone
left for Christmas,
and the Falcon
she made Raymond
keep the chains on
all year round
kept its nose
toward the road.
But Grandpa,
resting in the roots,
wouldn't quit
that foolishness.
He called her
when she wasn't
looking and he'd say
"Old sow, get down —
come see how slick
a crawler gets around . . ."
Grandma heard
the squirrels grinding
walnuts on the win-
dow sill, she heard,
way out back,
the deer come lick
the salt block too.

"I can hear most
anything . . . but Gramps,"
she said, "is gone
and he don't need
to talk to me
like that."

TOADS IN THE GREENHOUSE

When the scale were sucking
the life from my orchids,
I imported hundreds
of ladybugs into my life, —
blessing their tickle
among the sobered,
applauding the sparkle
they rendered to wrinkle
and droop. But soon these
ladies were snapped
away by the quick
sticky tongues of my toads,
whom I also had
affection for.
        Stuck,
I had to keep the leaves
breathing myself, washing
them off with soap and water, —
telling the toads when they
lumbered over to squat and watch
that what they saw was
what they saw. As always their faces
said: *We are simply here — two beauties
in a world gone buggy.*
And so they continued to lumber over,
keeping their mugs at the ready.

Summer began to steady itself
against autumn, my strongest spider
moved slower and slower
up in her corner, the ants
seemed to have scrammed for good.
Only the sluggish and slimy slugs,
I thought, kept the toads going.

I started leaving angleworms out
on a piece of musty pine
they liked, making sure
the worms were lively.
These little squiggles, they replied,
are adequate.
        Every night they'd
either be perched on the pine,
waiting, or hopping toward it.
I saw they were losing
their skins, scratching at the tough
places it wouldn't come off.
Then one night in a dream
they revealed themselves as uncles,
a wee bit hung over:
honey bees, they gargled,
bring us honey bees.
I ran toward them, my hands
brimming with mud, my feet freezing.
No, they said; *the sweetness,*
the sweetness . . .

In the morning frost had come —
and in the greenhouse, each to a pot,
the toads had burrowed down
among the roots;
I saw their noses briefly —
and then like deliberate
wonderful fish,
like prairie dogs,
or like uncles who can't quit
chasing the ladies,
they were gone.

BREAKING BONES

Sliding straight on mud
into third in sneakers
and partly hooking your foot
and partly trying to fly
ungainly is one way.

Another is playing Tarzan in the barn,
bareback or not it doesn't matter,
the crucial maneuver is beautiful Jane
about to be eaten limb from limb
across that passage you call a river, only
your grip slips
on the rope you call a vine
and landing, dazed, it's not
a school of piranha you feel
but something inside.

A third, if you've picked up
wearing a chip on your shoulder,
is one night stopping a hood's
chain with your wrist —
which in turn stops you
from snapping off
curves for a while.

So you learn something
and meanwhile get older,
knowing your chances of leading the league
are as slim as dropping from branches
to rescue the greenest girl around,
or setting the fastest gun on his can

— and yet, on certain days
when your ribs and the weather
have never felt better
and somewhere inside you've picked up a sign
you can't shake off,
you fill your lungs
and take off like a fool in love, gulping
dust and moonlight, kisses, phlegm,
pumping and flailing the air
until the air says *stop*
until the dirt says *here, take me*
and with everything
and nothing in your arms
you do.

POEM

My daughter and I lie in the snow
 beating our wings
and making breath — the sky
 slings it away.

Underneath, she says, is summer,
 underneath are all the fish
and cricket bones
 and where we go to die.

Once, I remember, I captured
 three minnows
and kept them hid in Dixie cups
 until they froze.

Later I tucked them under my pillow
 like teeth,
praying to God for a penny each.
 — Spiders sleep

all winter, too, she says,
 and bears in holes
and nobody knows
 where to find them.

A bouncing dog caught by the Union Pacific
 comes back.
 And my Uncle Stanley who quit
 seeing us

beating his cancer like Tarzan.
 And a woman
squeezing her eyes in the City of Angels,
 her amber tongue

stuck out for dope.   — If I ever
    walked across the sky,
  she says, I would grab a branch.
    If I ever walked across the sky.

We stop . . . and watch our breath.
    The sky slings it away.
  Later we look
    for a new patch of snow.

PITT POETRY SERIES

Paul Zimmer, General Editor

Dannie Abse, *Collected Poems*
Adonis, *The Blood of Adonis*
Jack Anderson, *The Invention of New Jersey*
Jack Anderson, *Toward the Liberation of the Left Hand*
Jon Anderson, *Death & Friends*
Jon Anderson, *In Sepia*
Jon Anderson, *Looking for Jonathan*
John Balaban, *After Our War*
Gerald W. Barrax, *Another Kind of Rain*
Robert Coles, *A Festering Sweetness: Poems of American People*
Leo Connellan, *First Selected Poems*
Michael Culross, *The Lost Heroes*
Fazıl Hüsnü Dağlarca, *Selected Poems*
James Den Boer, *Learning the Way*
James Den Boer, *Trying to Come Apart*
Norman Dubie, *Alehouse Sonnets*
Norman Dubie, *In the Dead of the Night*
Odysseus Elytis, *The Axion Esti*
John Engels, *Blood Mountain*
John Engels, *The Homer Mitchell Place*
John Engels, *Signals from the Safety Coffin*
Abbie Huston Evans, *Collected Poems*
Brendan Galvin, *The Minutes No One Owns*
Brendan Galvin, *No Time for Good Reasons*
Gary Gildner, *Digging for Indians*
Gary Gildner, *First Practice*
Gary Gildner, *Nails*
Gary Gildner, *The Runner*
Mark Halperin, *Backroads*
Michael S. Harper, *Dear John, Dear Coltrane*
Michael S. Harper, *Song: I Want a Witness*
Samuel Hazo, *Blood Rights*
Samuel Hazo, *Once for the Last Bandit: New and Previous Poems*
Samuel Hazo, *Quartered*
Gwen Head, *Special Effects*
Milne Holton and Graham W. Reid, eds., *Reading the Ashes: An Anthology of the Poetry of Modern Macedonia*
Milne Holton and Paul Vangelisti, eds., *The New Polish Poetry: A Bilingual Collection*
Shirley Kaufman, *The Floor Keeps Turning*

Shirley Kaufman, *Gold Country*
Abba Kovner, *A Canopy in the Desert: Selected Poems*
Paul-Marie Lapointe, *The Terror of the Snows: Selected Poems*
Larry Levis, *Wrecking Crew*
Jim Lindsey, *In Lieu of Mecca*
Tom Lowenstein, tr., *Eskimo Poems from Canada and Greenland*
Archibald MacLeish, *The Great American Fourth of July Parade*
Peter Meinke, *The Night Train and The Golden Bird*
Judith Minty, *Lake Songs and Other Fears*
James Moore, *The New Body*
Carol Muske, *Camouflage*
Gregory Pape, *Border Crossings*
Thomas Rabbitt, *Exile*
Belle Randall, *101 Different Ways of Playing Solitaire and Other Poems*
Ed Roberson, *Etai-Eken*
Ed Roberson, *When Thy King Is A Boy*
Eugene Ruggles, *The Lifeguard in the Snow*
Dennis Scott, *Uncle Time*
Herbert Scott, *Groceries*
Richard Shelton, *Of All the Dirty Words*
Richard Shelton, *The Tattooed Desert*
Richard Shelton, *You Can't Have Everything*
Gary Soto, *The Elements of San Joaquin*
David Steingass, *American Handbook*
David Steingass, *Body Compass*
Tomas Tranströmer, *Windows & Stones: Selected Poems*
Alberta T. Turner, *Learning to Count*
Alberta T. Turner, *Lid and Spoon*
Marc Weber, *48 Small Poems*
David P. Young, *Sweating Out the Winter*

*T*HIS first edition of

THE RUNNER

consists of fifteen hundred copies

in paper cover, five hundred copies

hardbound in boards,

and fifty specially bound copies

numbered and signed by the author.